Joe Tallarigo

Keep the Music Playing

Joe Tallarigo

All rights reserved. No part of this book may be reproduced without the written consent of the author.

Written and designed by Joe Tallarigo

Copyright © 2019

Published by Twin Hills Publishing LLC

ISBN: 978-1-7329930-0-6

To buy copies of Joe's books visit joesbook.webs.com

Joe Tallarigo

A word from the Author

2019 will be the twentieth anniversary of three important events that would shape my life and my poetry writing.

In the Spring of 1999, my aunt Mary invited my brother and I over to her apartment in Price Hill. She would order us our own large pizzas and two-liter of Cokes. As I ate my pizza, I would watch country music videos on CMT or GAC. It was my first exposure to country music, and seeing the singers, instead of just hearing them on radio, gave me a connection that made me want to see them perform when they came to my town.

In June of 1999, I graduated from Saint Lawrence Elementary school in Price Hill. It was a great eight-year experience in private school, and made many great friends and a lot of memories. But unlike most of my classmates I had moved to Delhi in 1997 so that my brother and I could attend Oak Hills High School.

On September 7, 1999 I became a freshman at Oak Hills. In 2001 I wrote my first poem after lunch. I wrote over forty poems by the time I graduated in 2003.

****

Music is a huge part of my life. In all honesty I never studied poetry in my life. I learnt how to write from listening to my favorite singers on cd on my cd player with earbuds. I carefully listened how the songwriters used words and phrases, and how they constructed their songs, and how they told the story of the song.
My first cd's I listened to were Celine Dion, The Eagles, Bryan Adams, Rod Stewart, Phil Collins and Journey but it wasn't until I began listening to cd's by Hank William Senior, Vern Gosdin, Johnny Cash, Tim McGraw and Darryl Worley my poems became more personal and more of the story telling type.

Keep the Music Playing

In 2000, I began following my local country music station B-105 and they hosted a lot of events where they would bring in up and coming country singers. From 2000-2009 I went to over fifty-concerts, met a lot of the singers, and gained knowledge and inspiration on what country music was from going to the concerts.

It truly felt like the universe was giving me the key to how songwriting and performing worked and I harnessed the power to write from the energy I was feeling and hearing at the concerts.

In 2018, I began performing my poetry at Common Roots, a bar in Price Hill, that hosts Open Mic night where talented singers and poets perform locally. I also had the pleasure of reading my poetry with the new Cincinnati Poet Laureate Manuel Iris, who is bringing poets together in Cincinnati for monthly theme readings.

Joe Tallarigo

Acknowledgements

Childhood Friends on Dewey: I can't believe it's been thirty years since we played baseball, football, tag, and hide and seek in Radel's Funeral Home lot and hanging out at each other's houses. We sure made a lot of great memories in the 1990's.

Saint Lawrence Classmates: It's been twenty years since we graduated. I hope everyone is chasing their dreams and doing well. We sure had a lot of fun going to Camp Kern and singing Christmas Carols to nursing home residents, and in third grade we had to hide under the tables in the lunchroom when the tornado came roaring through Price Hill. I Still remember the school dances, and singing together at our eighth-grade graduation mass.

B-105 Country Music Station: For all the program directors, and DJ's who bring joy to the fans at the concerts and various other events around Cincinnati. Thanks for bringing in the country music singers for decades and allowing fans to be able to meet them and being so gracious to your listeners.

Mary Spurlock: Rest in Peace. You taught our bible study group so much about the bible and its meaning in the eight years it was held at your house. I will miss our talks before bible study. We will see you one day again in Heaven.

Pepper: You were my first dog that I took home when I was eighteen years old. I still remember the night I took you home, how you jumped up and down every time I walked by your cage, trying to decide what dog I wanted to take home from the SPCA. I finally chose you. From 2002-2016 you were a wonderful travelling companion going to East Fork Lake, Bowling Green, Ohio and around Cincinnati. I will see you on the other side.

Robin and Joani Lacy: My favorite local musicians, and great friends who brings the New Orleans and Cajun Music to Cincinnati.

Price Hill Arts Council: I don't think I would have rediscovered my Price Hill roots had I not join in 2016.
We are slowly bringing the arts back to Price Hill, but I believe 2019 will be our break-out year for us and for the other residential artists and writers.

Voice Actors and Actresses: Thank you for making not only my childhood, but for all children and adults who watched your characters on television and in movies and for entertaining us for decades.

My Fellow Poets: Keep on writing and performing and inspiring others to write. To perform with each of you is an honor and I enjoy reading and hearing your perspective on life and events.

Joe Tallarigo

Chapter One:

Childhood Days

(me in 1990)

Ode to the 1990's

I started kindergarten in August of 1990
Reds swept the A's in the World Series
Disney Gummi Bears, Rescue Rangers, TaleSpin, Ducktales
were my favorite cartoons
Wilson Phillips ruled the airwaves
Nasa launched The Hubble Telescope into space
and the decade was just beginning

Dinosaurs, Clarissa Explains it All, Darkwing Duck,
Doug, Rugrats, Ren and Stimpy, all premiered in 1991
at the movies we watched Robin Hood Prince of Thieves,
Beethoven, Beauty and the Beast, Thelma and Louise
at home we were playing video games
on our Nintendo consoles

In 1993, Joe Carter lived out every boy's dream
when he hit a home-run to win the World Series
baseball stopped in 1994 due to the strike
but resumed in 1995 and Cal Ripken Jr passed Lou Gehrig
for playing in most consecutive games without a day off
then in 1998 came the great home-run chase
between Mark McGwire and Sammy Sosa

In between Animaniacs made us laugh
Sega, Playstation, Pogs, Beanie Babies, Tickle me Elmo
Titanic and "My Heart Will Go On" swept the world
Jodie Sweetin was my dream girl
Goosebumps, Are you Afraid of the Dark
gave kids scares and nightmares
The X-Files made us want to believe
the truth was out there

In 1999, it was A/S/L in chatrooms
dial-up internet, Ask Jeeves was my search engine
Y2K will our computers crash
on TV Ed, Edd, and Eddy, So Weird, Futurama,
Family Guy, Spongebob Squarepants, all premiered
I graduated from grade school that Spring
began high school that Fall
as the decade ended
we wondered what the 2000's would bring.

(Me with Mark McGwire)

Saturday's

Saturday mornings I rushed out of bed
down to the kitchen, open up the cabinets
for the sugary goodness in the cartoon cardboard boxes
hoping my brother and sister didn't get the toy first
or left behind only a handful of cereal
I needed at least two bowls
to watch the cartoons on TV

Saturday's, the only full day of freedom as a kid
a day to do what I wanted
didn't have to worry about school
or dress up to go to church
a free day to play with my toys, video games
and hang out with my friends
if it didn't rain

Sometimes my mom took me shopping
at Swallens, Woolworths, Thriftway, and K-Mart
I joined my school's baseball team
taking the field with my friends
with the determination to win the championship game
my taste in activities began to change
but one thing remained the same

Saturday's, the only full day of freedom as a kid
a day to do what I wanted
didn't have to worry about school
or dress up to go to church
a free day to play with my toys, video games
and hang out with my friends
if it didn't rain.

Grandparent's Houses

(Me and my brother)

On my dad's side
our grandma would put out Mr. T's Pizza, chips,
fruit snacks, and bowls of ice cream
for my brother and I to eat
my grandpa would sit in his favorite chair
wearing a Harry Caray T-shirt
while watching the Chicago Cubs on WGN

Sometimes we would put on parades and they would join in
other times we played hide and seek with our cousins
or pretend that we opened up a general store
in their kitchen pantry
outside we played baseball
losing the balls in the neighbor's hedges as if we were playing at
Wrigley Field

Keep the Music Playing

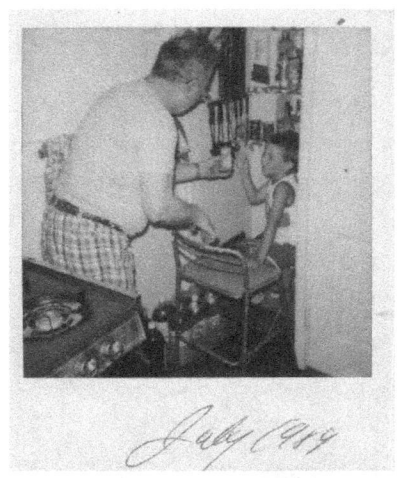

(Country Store)

On my mom's side
my brother and I spent our time
playing with Play-Doh and action figures at my grandma's kitchen table
she would make us chocolate milk
from the metal Nestle Quik cans
or Kool-Aid from the packets
while serving us soft baked chocolate chip cookies

Outside we played on a slip and slide
and had to dodge her rose bushes
other times we went to the basement
when the tornado sirens blared
we'd play pool
as we waited for the storms to pass

At both houses our families got together
for birthdays and holidays
at Halloween we'd walk around their neighborhoods
and on Christmas Day everyone exchanged gifts.

Joe Tallarigo

My grandma's house on my mom's side

(Me and my brother at my grandma's counter)

(My grandma, my brother, and I)

My grandparents on my dad's side

Joe Tallarigo

My Price Hill Days

I went swimming at Phillips Swim Club and Oskamps Pool
bought soft dough pretzels, Airheads, Icee's after school
played two-square, football, hide and seek
with my brother and my friends on the street
I walked to Rally's, Long John Silvers
when I wanted something to eat

My parents bought my school uniforms at Huber's
I went to Doctor Ratterman's when I was sick
he played football at Notre Dame
Friday nights I spent the night at my cousin's house
we rented movies, played with toys, and video games
or made up our own scary adventures

When it snowed I took my toys outside
held races between them on the slide
I went roller skating at Western Rollerama
my mom took us to the Laundromat on Warsaw
my brother and I played the arcade games
as our clothes washed and dried

I watched the Thanksgiving parade from
Radels Funeral Home parking lot
watching the floats and Santa go by
then I'd get ready to go to my aunts and uncles
to have a feast of pasta and turkey and dessert
and play football with my cousins
and his neighbors.

(My grandma, mom, me, and my sister at Phillips Swim Club)

(Snow races with my toys on my slide)

Joe Tallarigo

Round and Round

Every weekend the DJ at the roller rink played cupid
as he turned the lights down low
announced that everyone needed a partner
for the next two songs
everyone scrambled to find a hand to hold
I walked up to you as you waited on the bench
you said yes when I asked if you'd like to skate with me

Round and round we went
going slow, keeping steady
so we didn't trip and fall
but if we had, I bet we would have had a good laugh
I wondered if you noticed that my hand was sweaty
or were you caught up in the moment to even notice
as the disco ball and us
went round and round

Was it the songs, your touch
your smile, or that we were young
that made me want to continue to hold your hand
even though the slow songs had ended
there was something about having wheels on my feet
going slow and steady
that made my heart skip a beat

Round and round we went
going slow, keeping steady
so we didn't trip and fall
but if we had, I bet we would have had a good laugh
I wondered if you noticed that my hand was sweaty
or were you caught up in the moment to even notice
as the disco ball and us
went round and round.

Eagles

We became of age, eager to take what we learnt
to become successful in the new world
we were about to enter
our wings were spread, we were ready to soar
over the rivers, trees, and mountains

Though we were no longer the top dogs
since we were now back at the bottom as freshmen
but as long we stood side by side
we could fly to the sky
and motivate each other to chase our dreams

Some left the convocation
to new destinations and locations
we told them our goodbyes with hugs and tears
we wished them well
and prayed the future would treat them kind

We wore our red and gold with pride
we worked together as a team
made our parents and teachers proud
as our eight years together came to an end
we swore we would be friends forever

Now twenty years have come and gone
since we've graduated
sometimes it feels like a lifetime ago
that we were young and eager
to explore the new world we were about to enter.

Joe Tallarigo

Saint Lawrence Days

(First Day of Kindergarten)

(After Church Service)

Westside Festivals

You can win cakes, snacks, or flowers
spend a dollar to win twenty-five dollars
gamble on the rip-offs, the big six
sit and listen to the local bands on stage
kids play the duck pond, tic-tac-roll
and ride the carnival rides
everyone dreams of winning the grand prize

You'll run into old friends and neighbors
spend time catching up and reminiscing
teens walk around the booths
boys try to win their girls a teddy bear
adults play poker and black jack
grab some pizza, hot dog, or hamburger for dinner

Say hello to your former teachers working the booths
spend a few dollars on the raffle baskets
that catches your eye
it's only money and goes to a good cause

There's no shortage of Westside Festivals
every weekend from May to October
a church or community
sets up the red and white tents
for everyone to come and have fun.

Joe Tallarigo

Magic Eight Ball

Remember in our younger days
when we took the magic eight ball predicted as gospel
sometimes it cheated us, other times it treated us well
now as a man I consult my wife to decide what I should do
but back then right or wrong
it didn't matter to us
because in the Magic Eight Ball
we had put in our trust

Magic Eight Ball who knew all
led us on crazy adventures
got us in trouble, I lost out on girlfriends
since it answered ask again later
I often wished for snow but told me no
yes, was answered when asked if I should sneak out
and paint the town red

One long weekend in particular
my friends and I went camping at a lake near our house
we took pop, snacks, our fishing poles
but didn't tell our parents
they were mad as hell
asked why we would do such a thing
we replied the Magic Eight Ball told us to
when we asked if we should get away for the weekend

A few days later I came home from school
found my Magic Eight Ball was gone
it taught me not to sneak out with my friends
and I should have taken chances
asking the girls to the school dances
since we either strike gold or catch hell
for the things that we do
but those glory days of the Magic Eight Ball
were a lot of fun.

Long Out

It's the bottom of the ninth inning
with my teammate on first, there's two outs
if I can drive the ball into the gap
and he scores we can at least tie
but a home-run wins the game

The pitcher grits his teeth
waiting for the catcher to give the right sign
he nods his head, winds up, releases the ball
I swing my bat and connect
the ball goes sailing through the air

The crowd stands and cheers
then they go silent
as the ball gets lost in the lights
I round first base and keep going
until the ball lands somewhere in the stadium

The right fielder moves far back as he can
he runs out of real estate
as the ball comes back into view
a smile creeps on my face
I may have won the game
with my first career home-run

But the right fielder puts up his glove
jumps as high as he can
the ball lands in the leather
the crowd let's out a loud cry
I could hear their hearts breaking
as I just hit a long out to end the game.

Joe Tallarigo

Hot Air Balloon

Rising high in the red, purple, orange sky
on a hot, hazy, summer night
amongst other colorful cloth canvases
seeing the world as if I was a bird
we're higher than the mountains and planes
everything seems so surreal
from inside this wicker basket

I pray no gusts of wind will blow
and causes us to go off course
I want our journey to be smooth
this might be our only chance up here
so enjoy this view
I'll take some pictures that I can make into postcards
then I can sell them

Everyone looks like ants, the pastures look greener
the rivers truly do bend as they flow
look at the other balloons as they glow
as the full moon begins to rise
it's now getting cold being up so high
but I'm enjoying the ride
though I'm afraid of heights

I pray no gusts of wind will blow
and causes us to go off course
I want our journey to be smooth
this might be our only chance up here
so enjoy this view
I'll take some pictures that I can make into postcards
then I can sell them.

A December to Remember (2009)

The fun began on Black Friday
my parents took the grandkids and me downtown
to watch the city official's light up the Christmas tree
and watch the fireworks on Fountain Square
then they spent the night to help us decorate for Christmas

The weekend of the eleventh began with a
pasta dinner with my parents and friends
the next day I spent the night at my friend's house
and helped them decorate for Christmas
then went to church with them the next day
then watched their daughter on my birthday

The following weekend my cousin, brother, sister-in-law
came into town
around midnight snow began to fall
by Four A.M. we built a snowman
to greet the rest of the family
when they came over later in the day
to celebrate Christmas

The next day I was in Bowling Green, Ohio
with my brother and sister-in-law
on Christmas day our parents came up
we played games, exchanged, and opened gifts
then the following week I took my friends kids
to Sharonville Woods
to see their Christmas light display

It was a December to remember
never to be repeated
but the memories remain with me every Christmas.

Joe Tallarigo

The Snowman we Built

Kentucky Blue

No sweeter words were spoken
when she said you were the best thing
that ever happened to me
when we met in the blue fields of Kentucky

We spent our summer nights
counting the stars and making wishes
as we laid beneath the Lexington sky
in the blue fields of Kentucky

Red is the color of Love
but for me and you
its Kentucky Blue

No sweeter words were spoken
when she said you were the best thing
that ever happened to me
when we met in the blue fields of Kentucky

Soon we were just a memory
blowing through the trees
in the blue fields of Kentucky.

Joe Tallarigo

Dreams I didn't Chase

My grandpa had dreams that he'd see me
put on a gold helmet, navy-blue jersey
and take the field as a wide receiver
for the Notre Dame Fighting Irish
he would cheer and be proud when I scored a touchdown
but he passed away in 1997 when I was twelve years old
and I didn't chase the dreams he had for me

In 1989, when I was five years old
I got interested in the weather
when the temperatures dropped below zero
I enjoyed the severe storms that brought tornadoes
and big snowstorms that dropped over a foot of snow
I had over fifty VHS tapes of the local and national weather
by the time I was thirteen years old
thought I would be a meteorologist when I grew up
but I never chased that dream

(my brother, me, and dad at Notre Dame)

Keep the Music Playing

My favorite baseball player is Ryne Sandberg
who wore number twenty-three for the Chicago Cubs
and when I played baseball for Saint Lawrence
I wore number twenty-three
and hoped that one day I would take the field as a Cub
and follow in his footsteps
but I never chased that dream

In 1996, I began writing for my school newspaper
then moved onto writing paranormal stories in 1998
in 2001, I began writing poetry
and it's the only thing that stuck with me
I'm now going on twenty-three years
putting words on paper that tells the story
about dreams I didn't chase.

(My dad, me, Ryne Sandberg, and my Grandpa)

Joe Tallarigo

Me in my Baseball Uniform

Memories, Pictures, and Guitars

I've lived a third of my life
hanging out and working with great people
that I'm proud to call my friends
we've made special memories
like the nights we stayed up late
writing and creating scripts for our movies
reading our poetry across the city
or going to dinner after a hard day's work

I'm a young soul trying to keep my innocence
I've been a hero, a bad guy
I have a rambling spirit stuck in a reluctant body
I want to go to Nashville and sing my songs
then head down to the islands
and open up my own bar
hoist a cold drink in my hand
to toast my memories, pictures, and guitars

I love taking photos of my family and friends
and places I've traveled to
then making them into collages
hang them on my walls
reminding me of where I've been
and all the fun we had

I'm a young soul trying to keep my innocence
I've been a hero, a bad guy
I have a rambling spirit stuck in a reluctant body
I want to go to Nashville and sing my songs
then head down to the islands
and open up my own bar
hoist a cold drink in my hand
to toast my memories, pictures, and guitars

Time is slipping away
just like my dreams
I've enjoyed my trips around the sun
and all the laughs we had
like the time I had my guitar in my hand
when the chair I was sitting in collapsed
the guitar went up in the air
but still managed to catch it with my hands
when it fell to the ground
but I broke a few ribs from the collapse
then there was the time in Chicago
my dad lost his wallet in a taxi
and it ended up in Milwaukee
last but not least
I was on vacation at Deer Creek
I jumped in the lake with my new camera and phone
that I had left in my pocket
and ruined both

It's memories, pictures, and guitars
that makes the world go round and round.

Chapter Two

Tonight, the Country Called Me

Joe Tallarigo

Tonight, the Country Called Me

Tonight, the country called me
told me about its rich history
starting with Jimmie Rodgers and the Carter Family
it told me about the Opry
and all the stars to see in Nashville Tennessee

Tonight, the country called me
said everyone is welcome, but not everyone stays
some cross over and make pop songs
but we welcome them back with open arms
it's hard to make everyone happy
tonight, the country called me

Tonight, the country called me
asked me if I heard Patsy Cline sing "Crazy"
or Ernest Tubb's "Journey's End"
he then asked how I felt about steel guitars
twin fiddles and Bon Jovi
tonight, the country called me

Tonight, the country called me
said there are open roads, trucks, nice folks
you can catch a ride to Folsom Prison
on a long black train
or visit the Caribbean
with Kenny Chesney
tonight, the country called me.

Keep the Music Playing

My Country Music History

From 1999 to 2002 on Saturday nights
I'd sit on my aunt's couch in her apartment
I'd eat a large cheese pizza and drink a two-liter of coke
watching the newest country music videos on CMT
Sawyer Brown, Toby Keith, Sara Evans, Rascal Flatts,
Brooks and Dunn, Collin Raye, Shania Twain, Clint Black,
Terri Clark, Tim McGraw, Faith Hill, Kenny Chesney,
George Strait, Alan Jackson, Phil Vassar, Brad Paisley
were the first singers I discovered
in my country music history

In 2000, I went to my first Taste of Cincinnati
B-105 would bring in the newest singers from Nashville
I went down every Memorial Day weekend until 2009
I got to meet Shedaisy, Darryl Worley, Trick Pony,
Dusty Drake, Dierks Bentley, Emerson Drive,
Joey and Rory, Luke Bryan and Miranda Lambert
2001 was the summer of fun
Met a DJ nicknamed Stattman
gave me tickets to Jamming in the Country
I met Tim Rushlow and Joe Diffie
at their concerts at the Kentucky Speedway
and that December Steve Holy wore my cowboy hat on stage
and sang Happy Birthday to me
adding to my country music history

I met Kenny Chesney in 2002, before he was a big star
my mom and I met Vince Gill and Amy Grant in 2003
in 2005 I shook George Strait's hand
as he walked to the stage
I met Richie McDonald of Lonestar in 2007
went to Nashville in 2009 and met Ronnie Dunn
since 2010 going to concerts
and meeting singers have slowed down
but I still enjoy the music I grew up on
and enjoy sharing my country music history.

(Joe Diffie and Me)

(Kenny Chesney)

Keep the Music Playing

(Me with Phil Vassar)

(Rory, Joey, and Me)
(Rest in peace Joey)

Joe Tallarigo

(Me with B-105 DJ Stattman)

(Me with Steve Holy)

Country Home

Peaches and apples grow on trees
bees buzz in the summer breeze
roses grow along white picket fences
dogs howl at the moon
mails delivered by nine
neighbors come over for coffee and small talk

In my country home
everyone is welcome
it's not too big, not too small
pictures of my family decorate the walls
come on in you'll have ball

My wife decorated the kitchen in green
our living room has a cabin feel
there's a fireplace to keep us warm
and a radio to listen to country music
but there's no tv

In my country home
everyone is welcome
it's not too big, not too small
pictures of my family decorate the walls
come on in you'll have ball

It's my mansion
built on simplicity
it's nothing too fancy
it's just right
for an old country soul like me.

Joe Tallarigo

Pies

There are slices of cherry, blueberry, apple pies
waiting to be served in diners after lunch or dinner
on little plates, don't feel guilty dig right in
enjoy the fruity, creamy dessert while the going is good
you're allowed to treat yourself every now and then

Women are busy cooking in their kitchens
preparing for their holiday guests
they have ingredients for
pumpkin, sweet potato, and rhubarb pies
the sweet aroma will linger in their houses
long after they've been eaten

To stay cool on hot summer days
you can't go wrong with key lime pie
with a margarita to chase it down
then relax in a hammock
and take a nap in the sunshine

Girls, if you want to get to my heart
set out a slice of Boston or chocolate cream pie
with whipped cream and cherry on top
I'll be right over with my fork and knife
I'll savor each bite

Pies, pies, pies
so many to choose from and make
some are for every day, some made special for holidays
enjoy a slice every now and then
life wouldn't be the same
if there were no pies for dessert.

Jimmy's Fishing Hole

In the deep hollers of North Carolina
there's a place the boys and men know
where the fish are always biting
they can feed their families for days
with all the fish they catch
it's known as Jimmy's fishing hole

Jimmy wasn't the smartest guy
he made moonshine and was always in trouble with the law
but it's said one September night in 1929
he conjured up a potion that made the fish always bite
when he poured it in the lake near his house
to this day no one knows how he made it
all they know is when they throw out their lines
the fish will always bite

All the boys in school stare at the clock
counting down the hours until the final bell at three
so they can take their poles, their girls
to catch a fish, steal a kiss
down at Jimmy's fishing hole

In the deep hollers of North Carolina
there's a place the boys and men know of
where the fish are always biting
they can feed their families for days
with all the fish they catch
it's known as Jimmy's fishing hole.

Joe Tallarigo

Let's Pray the Fish are Biting

I have four hundred dollars of fishing gear
I've wanted to try out all year
today looks like a good day as any
to go to Swanson's Lake
before we leave
let's pray the fish are biting
and the mosquitoes aren't

We can take a cooler of beer, a grill
so we can cook what we catch
as we watch the sun set
before we throw out our lines
let's pray the fish are biting
and the mosquitoes aren't

It'll just be you and me on still waters
we'll talk about your mother and father
have all the conversations we've been saving for a rainy day
like when are we going to start our own family
before we throw out our lines
let's pray the fish are biting
and the mosquitoes aren't

I have four hundred dollars of fishing gear
I've wanted to try out all year
today looks like a good day as any
to go to Swanson's Lake
before we leave
let's pray the fish are biting
and the mosquitoes aren't.

If I was a Deer Hunter

If I was a deer hunter
I'd be gone for days
on the hunt for the biggest buck
I'd send my wife postcards from my tree stand
writing it's cold and lonely wish you were here
but I've got to go now and watch for the deer

If I was a deer hunter
I'd wear camouflage
you wouldn't recognize me
as I track the bucks and does through the snow
people may think its weird to sit in a tree all day
waiting on something that may never come
but for me it's the thrill of the hunt

If I was a deer hunter
I'd build me a camp
for my friends
we'd lived there all winter
living off beef stew and Red Bull
hoping we all get a ten-point buck

But to tell you the truth
I only own a camera
which I like to point and shoot
capture the deer
in their natural habitat
I have a few photos of bucks and does hanging in frames
but my friends say it's not the same
as having deer heads mounted on my walls.

Joe Tallarigo

Buck at East Fork Lake

Butterfly Ridge

There's a place I know
where flowers bloom in an array of colors
rabbits and deer frolic in the clover
a crystal blue stream flows through the woods
the birds freely sing their songs without reprieve
while the butterflies play in the Spring breeze

You can sit on large rocks by the water
to stare at your reflection
to see who you really are
at night you'll never finish counting the stars
the moon provides adequate light
so you can take a midnight hike
and view the wildlife

There are many types of wild flowers to pick
to give to your lover
as you set out lunch
in the clover fields
while you eat
you can watch the deer scurry by

Feel the serenity as the butterflies fly by
view the sunset through the trees
thank God and give Him praise
for this wonderful day
and all the beauty he creates
up here on butterfly ridge.

Joe Tallarigo

Butterfly on a Flower

Ducks on the Pond
(Gibb's Song)

He runs to the front door and barks
then bolts into my bedroom and hops on my bed
he wants me to put his leash on
then to get in the car and drive to our local park
to visit the geese and ducks on the pond

He watches the ducks waddle and eat
while the geese walk around the parking lot
his eyes light up when they walk towards him
he sees them as his friends and wants to hang out with them
I believe he thinks they are other dogs

When winter comes, he stares out the front window
I can hear him whimpering from behind the curtains
he doesn't understand why he can't get in the car
and go to the park
to visit the geese and ducks on the pond

He runs to the front door and barks
hoping I'll put his leash on
he'll drag me to the car
to drive to the park
and make sure his friends are staying warm

But I tell him they all flew South
they'll be back in the Spring
we'll have to wait for warmer weather
to visit his friends at the pond
but the waiting is no fun.

Joe Tallarigo

Gibbs looking at the ducks

Fishing and Flying

I was eleven years old fishing in Jackson's creek
when an airplane flew over the treetops
and caught my attention
I watched it fly into the sun
I ran home without my pole and the fish I caught
I said to my parents
I want to be a pilot, can I take flying lessons

Over the next few years I learnt how to take off and land
I studied the instruments as I racked up my miles
so I could earn my wings
I had little time for family and friends
and the things I used to do like fishing
but it was well worth it in the end

The day finally came I got my pilot's license
and years later I became an airplane captain
spending my days flying coast to coast
soon the stress caught up to me
and one day flying over Tennessee
I eyed a creek, like the one I used to fish in
I saw a little boy with his fishing pole
I looked away, then looked down again
and the little boy had disappeared

Then it hit me, I gave up everything
to follow my dreams now I wish I was still a boy
in Jackson's creek with my fishing pole and lures
with no stress, taking it day to day
but seeing that plane over the trees put ideas in my head
I'm now flying over streams and creeks
I should be fishing in.

Joe Tallarigo

Outside this Town

He lived in his grandparents' house
in a town with a population of seventy-five
went to school with a class of nine
took the girl he met in kindergarten
to his senior prom
then went to work at the country store

Outside this town has yet to be explored
never took the main road to highway 74
his roots are planted firmly in the ground
where his great-grandpa first toiled the soil
his dad says he's proud
and never thought of ever crossing the county line
we're born, work, live, and die
in this town

He heard L.A. was filled with stars
people express themselves in Nashville with guitars
Seattle is the Emerald city where dreams come true
but he doesn't have the wings to fly away

Outside this town has yet to be explored
never took the main road to highway 74
his roots are planted firmly in the ground
where his great-grandpa first toiled the soil
his dad says he's proud
and never thought of ever crossing the county line
we're born, work, live, and die
in this town.

Everyday Living

James kicks a pop can down the street
excited that it's the first day of Spring
he meets his friends at the park
where they'll play baseball until it gets dark

Sarah visits her longtime friend Elizabeth
helps plants flowers in Elizabeth's garden
then they have lemonade and cookies
as they talk about their summer plans

Tim is teaching his two sons
how to fish at the lake
with the new fishing poles he bought them
then they throw out their lines and wait for a bite

Mark and Stacey are on their first date
Sharon is in the woods taking photos of the wildlife
Pastor James is preparing his homily for Sunday
and Sheriff Grant is praying for a peaceful night

It's everyday living
waking up to sunshine
swinging on a front porch swing
having friends over for the weekend
saying "I do" to your bride
enjoying every minute trying new things
walking your dog around the block
it's everyday living at its best.

Joe Tallarigo

Rivertown

You can find me sitting on the edge of the fountain
in the town square
with my best friends
watching people toss coins in the water
making wishes that may or may not come true

We're just living in a river-town
where we enjoy watching the local bands perform every weekend
on the river front
kids are playing in their front yards
while their parents are grilling out

On the corner of Main Street is my favorite diner
I order their cheeseburger, fries, strawberry shake
and enjoy seeing Elaine's lovely smile
she always tells me one day she's going to be a huge star
if she can get to Hollywood

We're just living in a river-town
where we enjoy watching the local bands playing every weekend
on the river front
kids are playing in their front yards
while their parents are grilling out

Trains roll down the tracks
teens hang out in the barns
there's no big city in sight
you can spend the whole night
counting the stars
in a river-town.

16th Avenue

From my tenth-floor office window
I watch a woman hail a taxi
as she holds her packages stacked high to the sky
there's a young couple pushing a baby stroller
while a business man talks on his phone
I bet he's trying to seal the big deal

Here on sixteenth avenue, there's always a smiling face
checking out the shops and the latest deals
women gather in the salons
to catch up on the latest gossip
men play checkers in the park until it gets dark
everyone does their own thing
here on sixteenth avenue

A bus stops on the corner to pick kids up to take to school
a man lights up a cigarette while his wife window shops
she stares at a thousand-dollar dress she'll never buy
there are stray dogs chasing alley cats down the street
and the boys in blue patrol to keep the peace

Here on sixteenth avenue, there's always a smiling face
checking out the shops and the latest deals
women gather in the salons
to catch up on the latest gossip
men play checkers in the park until it gets dark
everyone does their own thing
here on sixteenth avenue.

Joe Tallarigo

Boulevard Dreams

There's an old oak tree that shades the ground
where the green grass grows
our children play on their swing set
we have an inground pool we swim in
a gazebo where we eat our dinners
and watch the sun set
on our Boulevard dreams

I'm not rich, but I'm not poor
I've been blessed to have a loving wife
two great kids who go to a private school
I tell them life isn't always easy
but if you have God and goals
then you're already on the right path
to your own Boulevard dreams

Our couch and chairs have been passed down since 1932
our good china is even older
our friends don't mind we like antiques
when they come over for a visit
like the good ole days gone by
when neighbors knew each other
I'm glad we live where we do

I'm not rich, but I'm not poor
I've been blessed to have a loving wife
two great kids who go to a private school
I tell them life isn't always easy
but if you have God and goals
then you're already on the right path
to your own Boulevard dreams.

Nitty Gritty

Life sure is funny
sometimes I'm city, sometimes I'm country
I live for today, make music all night long
I have a lot of soul in my body
but when it comes down to the nitty gritty
I'm pretty easy going

I love to fish and drink root beer
playing poker with my friends on Friday nights
Saturday's I'm shopping with my lady
Sunday's I'm watching the big games

Life sure is funny
sometimes I'm city, sometimes I'm country
I live for today, make music all night long
I have a lot of soul in my body
but when it comes down to the nitty gritty
I'm pretty easy going

I can't stand all these reality shows
with all the fake fights and drama
if you want reality
turn off your TV
and step outside

Life sure is funny
sometimes I'm city, sometimes I'm country
I live for today, make music all night long
I have a lot of soul in my body
but when it comes down to the nitty gritty
I'm pretty easy going.

Joe Tallarigo

Born Naked

We're all born naked
so why do we hide behind our clothes
our insecurities
time to shed our false identities
bring out who we really are
should we care how people look at us
we're all crazy and different in our own ways
and that's what makes us the same

We're all born naked
we all deserve peace, love, harmony
our place in the sun
we look for friends to share in the fun
but then we put our walls, give excuses
to why we're not number one
we start to care about what people think of us
believe we're not worthy as those on the covers of magazines
but remember they were born naked too

I get frustrated by money
everything feels out of place
I see a face in the mirror I don't recognize
I look tired and worn down from a job that tears me down
and have a boss who laughs all the way to the bank
having good times on my hard work and dime

We're all born naked
we all deserve peace, love, harmony
our place in the sun
we look for friends to share in the fun
but then we put our walls, give excuses
to why we're not number one
we start to care about what people think of us
believe we're not worthy as those on the covers of magazines
but remember they were born naked too

Keep the Music Playing

I'm going to be me
and they can shove it
if they don't like it
I'm breaking the chains, tearing down my cage
and bite the hands that fed me the line
that I wasn't good enough
they better watch out I'm on a mission
to prove them all wrong.

Joe Tallarigo

Man of my Time

Excuse me if I don't buy cd's
when I can download or stream a song
I hold onto my money
I have no faith in the banks or stock market
I don't root for the Cowboys
or the Bronx Bombers
they were once America's team
but things are changing, rearranging

I'm just a man of my time
things are more technical than practical
we have internet on our phones and watches
cars that run on electricity
it's overwhelming how far we've come along
I don't care for most of it
I'm just a man of my time

I like to play video game online
as my Nintendo and Sega collects dust
I sleep in on Saturday mornings
and I no longer buy cereal
since they no longer have prizes

I'm just a man of my time
things are more technical than practical
we have internet on our phones and watches
cars that run on electricity
it's overwhelming how far we've come along
I don't care for most of it
I'm just a man of my time

What would Van Gogh think of art today
using a computer mouse to paint and draw
what would Charlie Chaplin think of today's movies
what would the Wright Brother's think of today's airplanes

Keep the Music Playing

<pre>
       They were just men of their times
   when things were more practical than technical
          times were simpler back then
          but look how far we've come
            in a few hundred years
          I'm just a man of my time.
</pre>

Joe Tallarigo

Pocket Change

Gone are the days of lying in bed
wishing I had another hour to sleep
boss man wants the report on his desk by nine
but I only have happy hour on my mind
as I put on my suit, tie, and pants
I reach into my pockets and find

Pocket change
it was my time to party and unwind
but I had to pay my bills and rent
my paycheck sure didn't last long
I was hoping for one weekend of fun
guess I'll wait for my tax refund
because all I seem to have left after payday is
pocket change

Gone are the days of low paying jobs
and trying to get fired
I need overtime and higher pay
and if I'm really lucky I'll retire a millionaire
but it's the end of the month
and all I have left is

Pocket change
it was my time to party and unwind
but I had to pay my bills and rent
my paycheck sure didn't last long
I was hoping for one weekend of fun
guess I'll wait for my tax refund
because all I seem to have left after payday is
pocket change.

Chapter Three

Life Moments and Philosophies

Joe Tallarigo

Straight to Haggard

Love blooms in the Spring in the field of diamond rings
but many lies and alibis are told
underneath a whiskey moon and tequila stars
many great songs come from old guitars
that are played in honky-tonk bars
swinging doors, whiskey and gin
are my friends once again

When I'm blue and have nothing to do
I go straight to Haggard
listening to those sad country songs
it puts me in the mood
to hop onto a train and travel as a lonesome fugitive
change my name, live in a town
where no one knows who I am
and start my life a-new

I have my own bar stool, the bar keep is my friend
the patrons share in my misery
the jukebox plays Waylon and Jones
when I need to remember to toe the mark and walk the line
to kill time
I play darts alone

When I'm blue and have nothing to do
I go straight to Haggard
listening to those sad country songs
it puts me in the mood
to hop onto a train and travel as a lonesome fugitive
change my name, live in a town
where no one knows who I am
and start my life a-new.

Ode to George Strait

It's another "Honky-tonk Saturday night"
just "beyond the blue neon lights"
in "honkytonkville"
we'll be dancing and drinking all night long
to swinging country songs

There's a peddler selling "ocean front property"
by the "seashores of ole Mexico"
there's a "lonesome rodeo cowboy"
trying to make it to "Amarillo by morning"
drinking doesn't make it "right or wrong"

Alan he's my "designated drinker"
sometimes I get "carried away"
finding myself using pickup lines like
"heaven's missing an angel"
"I just want to dance with you"

I was bit by the "lovebug"
fell in love with a "high tone woman"
I found myself being "true"
then one day out of the "blue clear sky"
she came to me with "good news, bad news"

I found myself with a "fool hearted memory"
I vowed to take it "one night at a time"
now she "looks so good in love"
but that's as "far as it goes"
as I become "unwound"

Joe Tallarigo

Ode to George Strait Part 2

"The best day" came a few years later
when I found some "stars by the water"
she was the "real thing"
"Adalida" was her name
and love was her game

I was "living and living well"
down in "Marina Del Rey"
with my "infinite love"
"I crossed my heart"
"I'd never give it away"

"It's dance time in Texas"
other "Cowboys like us"
are "here for a good time"
all the way to the "heartland"
with the "brothers of the highway"

"Honk if you honky-tonk"
is our slogan
but this "cowboy has to ride away"
to settle on down
"somewhere down in Texas"

I'll live side by side with "all my exes"
"blame it on Mexico"
for my rodeo living
and blame the "80-proof tear stopper"
for my "troubadour" singing.

Western Skies and Honky-Tonks

He dreams of being a cowboy
riding, roping, competing in rodeo's
living on a thousand-acre ranch
but he's stuck on sixth avenue
a third-generation lawyer
living with his wife and son
in a huge four-bedroom house in the suburbs

He's seen the sunrise in Manhattan
but never a sunset in Wyoming
he's danced and dined in the fanciest of clubs
but never stepped into a honky-tonk
so every night he wishes upon a star
that one day he'll see Western skies and honky-tonks

As a kid his mom said cowboys never settle down
there's no money to be made
since the wild west days are over
so he takes on cases, makes good money
but he still yearns to ride away

He's seen the sunrise in Manhattan
but never a sunset in Wyoming
he's danced and dined in the fanciest of clubs
but never stepped into a honky-tonk
so every night he wishes upon a star
that one day he'll see Western skies and honky-tonks

He buys his son cowboy hats and boots
says one day they'll make it out West
sleep beneath the stars of a Western sky
and when his son turns twenty-one
they will throw back some cold ones
in a honky-tonk.

Joe Tallarigo

Cowgirl, Go get Him

Girl, I see all the signs
the way you look and twitch
doing anything you can think of
to get his attention
you want to call out his name but you can't say a word
every time he walks by

You ask his friends for his number
asks if he's going steady with another girl
come on, get on your horse
find the courage you have when you rope and ride
he's the same as any other man
why are you acting so shy

Cowgirl, go get him
wrap him in your arms, never let go
tell him you want him forever
put on your best smile
so he'll fall in love with you
go get him cowgirl
you have nothing to lose

You hide behind your insecurities
say you don't want to get hurt
if he's already seeing another girl
or say's he's not into you
but you'll never know if you don't ask
take the chance the next time he walks by
tell him what's on your mind

Cowgirl, go get him
wrap him in your arms, never let go
tell him you want him forever
put on your best smile
so he'll fall in love with you
go get him cowgirl
you have nothing to lose.

Forever is a Dream

Like a mountain stream
that flows peacefully
like the bees and butterflies
that glide in the Spring breeze
like the clouds
that travel high in the sky
I was chasing a feeling I couldn't see
kept reaching out to a belief
that love would be easy to find
to me forever is a dream

In a field of daisies and clover
I laid out beneath the sun
visualizing the magical moment
where I'd find the woman meant for me
we'd fall in love at first sight
but love is always one step ahead of me
to me forever is a dream

Then one day out of the blue
there she was, so young and carefree
I felt like lightning struck me
filling me with all kinds of emotions
didn't have a clue what to do

But she was patient, kind
made the world stood still
as she held out her hand
so that I could take hold
and in that moment
I knew I'd never let go

Joe Tallarigo

Forever seemed like a dream
one that I couldn't shake
I knew that one day
I'd finally feel all the emotions
that lovers and poets write and talk about
now life is moving slow
like a mountain stream
that flows peacefully
like the birds and the bees
that glide in the Spring breeze
like the clouds
that travel high in the sky
forever is no longer a dream
now that I have you next to me.

Living out a Sad Country Song

To say he was broken hearted would be an understatement
his hands shaking as he tried to light up his sixth cigarette
while asking the bartender for his fifth gin and whiskey
his eyes dried out from all his crying
he said I never smoked or drank before
but I've never been so depressed
never imagined I'd fully understand the feelings
and living out a sad country song

My heart is shattered into a million pieces
it hurts to breathe
my thoughts go back to the first day we met
and how I felt looking into her baby blue eyes
running my hands through her sandy blond hair
now I'm sitting here in the last place I thought I'd ever be
but it beats being home all alone
staring at my phone hoping that she calls

She was my first and only true love
now my better half is walking the streets
or taking a greyhound bus to the midnight sun
while I'm nursing this heartache from hell
I'm going to keep drinking until I'm numb from this pain
and I feel the rain pour down on me
like they say it does
in those sad country songs

My heart is shattered into a million pieces
it hurts to breathe
my thoughts go back to the first day we met
and how I felt looking into her baby blue eyes
running my hands through her sandy blond hair
now I'm sitting here in the last place I thought I'd ever be
but it beats being home all alone
staring at my phone hoping that she calls.

Joe Tallarigo

Tears

Tears are natural waterfalls from our eyes
when we're feeling happy or sad
tears are words we can't form
when we're choked up with emotions
tears are for those lonely in the night
for lovers hugging tight excited for the news
they're expecting a bundle of joy

Tears are for newborns to those over one hundred years old
no one is exempt from showing their emotions
crying is natural like breathing and sleeping
though there are some people who are good at keeping it hidden
then there are those who shed tears at the tiniest tender moments

Tears heal heartaches that life brings us
tears reveal the rainbow through the storms
tears help roses grow in the garden of hope
tears are free like hugs from friends

Tears are for newborns to those over one hundred years old
no one is exempt from showing their emotions
crying is natural like breathing and sleeping
though there are some people who are good at keeping it hidden
then there are those who shed tears at the tiniest tender moments

Tears are natural waterfalls from our eyes
come to me as you let them fall
I can see you could use a friend
come use my shoulder to cry on
and tell me about your problems.

A Good Glass of Wine

I believe women should take the time to relax and unwind
at the end of every night
to cozy up on the couch with the lights down low
reading a romantic tale or who done it mystery
while sipping a good glass of wine

I believe women should celebrate their accomplishments
with their good friends
life is too short not to acknowledge
when someone achieves their dreams
so lift up your glasses, give a toast
with a good glass of wine

I believe men and women can bond in one good night
sitting in a corner booth on their first date
talking about their likes and dislikes
having a laugh or two
as they wait for their food
a long night awaits them to see if a sparks form
but their nerves and worries can be calmed
with a good glass of wine

Celebrate life, the good times
or if you need to unwind
and need to let go from reality
pour yourself and have yourself
a good glass of wine.

Joe Tallarigo

Sun City Carnival

Four P.M. in the stadium parking lot
we have coolers of pop, food on the grill
our favorite summer songs blaring on the radio
other fans are stopping by
there's not a cloud in the sky
no chance of rain
but there's 100% chance of fun
at the Sun City Carnival

We come out by the thousands
from all over the country
girls are wearing bikini tops and cut-off jeans
boys are wearing cowboy hats and showing off their tans
we're all here to see the man
who sings about summer and life
and to have a good time
at the Sun City Carnival

He takes the stage, begins to sing his songs
all the girls scream and sing along
the boys take in the moment
the party is just beginning
I need to save some energy
since the concert ends at eleven
it feels like heaven
at the Sun City Carnival

Let your troubles take you away
forget about the stress at the office
we're not here to complain
this is the first official day of Summer
come on down, don't miss out on the fun
at the Sun City Carnival.

Tennessee Spirit

I love visiting the Smoky Mountains in the Fall
with red, orange, and yellow leaves lighting up the back roads
I gaze through the early misty fog drinking hot chocolate
on the cabin balcony
hoping to see a mama bear with her cubs
I enjoy taking the trolley into town
and shopping at the novelty stores
where I can buy t-shirts with different sayings
homemade soaps, chocolates, scented candles
while feeling the Tennessee spirit around me

Saturday's in the Fall
you'll find the college kids rooting for the Vols
I remember when Peyton Manning
led the team to 13-0 in 1998
in Nashville on Saturday nights the country singers
prepare for another performance at the Opry
it's been on the air since 1925
with the twang and steel guitars being heard
all around the world
while feeling the Tennessee spirit around you

In Memphis, millions of fans visit the house of Elvis
to see his life up close and feel the magic he gave us
he was gone too soon, but he sure made the girls swoon
another great country singer Conway Twitty
enjoyed singing love songs
he made it look easy to say what lovers wanted to say
and helped break the ice
on many first dates
while feeling the Tennessee spirit around them.

Joe Tallarigo

My Favorite Places in Gatlinburg

(my favorite ice cream parlor in Gatlinburg)

A Woman Like You

Smoky eyes, red blouse
standing behind me
in a sea of people
waiting for the concert to begin
I just happened to notice you
and the man you're with
he's a lucky guy and you make a good couple
but I've got to say

A woman like you seems out of place
here in the big city
you seem more of a New Orleans or island girl
with your gypsy soul
and carefree spirit
while projecting a southern charm
that makes it easy for someone like me
to talk to a woman like you

I wish I got your name
to put with your beautiful face
I see the way you dance with him
that kind of fun and love is hard to find
I bet that you're both cut from the same cloth
I'm happy you found your soulmate
but I have to say

A woman like you seems out of place
here in the big city
you seem more of a New Orleans or island girl
with your gypsy soul
and carefree spirit
while projecting a southern charm
that makes it easy for someone like me
to talk to a woman like you.

Joe Tallarigo

Rolling on the Nights

I saved up my money for a sunny day
told my friends I couldn't come out and play
since it's been too stormy and gray
for me to have fun but that's changed now

I hear the rodeo is in town
I want to see the clowns distract the bulls
the Reds are playing great baseball
hey, come on now
let's not waste any time
let's go out and have some fun

We can be rolling on the nights
invite all our friends
to Rick's BBQ Joint
order some fries and wings
play darts and pool
as we watch the Reds take on the Cardinals
we'll have the time of our lives
rolling on the nights

My youth is wasting away
hanging out in my dorm
chatting with my friends online
as we all study for our finals
and recalling our younger days when we hung out all night
what do you say we close our books
and have some fun

We can be rolling on the nights
invite all our friends
to Rick's BBQ Joint
order some fries and wings
play darts and pool
as we watch the Reds take on the Cardinals
we'll have the time of our lives
rolling on the nights.

Everyone is going to Florida

Everyone I know is traveling in cars or airplanes
making their way to the Sunshine state
summer break is in full swing
can you blame them for wanting to get away
to play in the sand and ocean
I wish I was crossing the Bama-Florida line
but I'm stuck here in Ohio

Everyone is now in Florida
posting their photos online
smiling as they pose on the piers
taking selfies with the cartoon characters
making lifetime memories
I wish I was in Orlando
walking the streets of Disney World

No tropical storms or hurricanes are in the forecast
honey, I have several vacation days coming my way
what do you say we start packing our suitcases
and have ourselves some fun
we can go out on a boat to see the manatee's
collect seashells we find on the beach
as we watch the sun set
doesn't that sound dreamy

Everyone is going to Florida
while I'm stuck here in Ohio.

Joe Tallarigo

Lost in my Thoughts

If you see me staring into space
know that I'm okay
I'm just observing the world around me
plotting my next poem
creating characters and what they might say
forming a world just for them
with my words

I'm always lost in my thoughts
daydreaming of what life could be like
but I sometimes get trapped in the webs I weave
writing for hours on end
other times I feel like a sailor on the sea
trying to find an island or country
that's yet to be explored
to claim it and make it my own

I'm also shy, I sweat the small talk
let's get straight to the point
unless you want to talk about our favorite hobbies
then I can go on for hours
and if you want to know how to write a poem
then I'm your man
I'll reveal my secrets
starting with

I'm always lost in my thoughts
daydreaming of what life could be like
but I sometimes get trapped in the webs I weave
writing for hours on end
other times I feel like a sailor on the sea
trying to find an island or country
that's yet to be explored
to claim it and make it my own.

My Philosophy

I might be young
but I've had my trips around the sun
I'm a jerk
when it comes to work
but I realized at an early age
it's not about the money we make
or how much of the pie we take

It's about the friends we have
the memories we make
the laughter, smiles, and tears
going to concerts and ballgames
it's not about fortune and fame
it's how we live
and go about each day

It's about the chances we take
the promises we break
that everyday isn't the same
it's fun to play in the rain
and the pain may never go away

It's not about the car we drive
It's how hard we try
It's alright for a guy to cry
It's alright to dance when there's no music
you sometimes have to lose
to earn some humility

I'm going to live life as I want
travel the world
flirt with the girls
not have life pass me by
or have people bring me down.

Joe Tallarigo

A Good Storm

A good storm every now and then
is good for the soul
let the wind take away the loose things
that we no longer need
let the rain pour down on you
make it feel as if you're being baptized
by Holy Water from Heaven above
let the lightning light up the dark sky
so you can see the truth
through the deceit and lies

The dark clouds make me smile
the bending of tree tops
let me know it's going to get wild
with open arms I bare my soul
ready to get cleansed
have my spirit renewed
so I can carry on
without a heavy load on my shoulder

A good storm every now and then
is good for the soul
let the wind take away the loose things
that we no longer need
let the rain pour down on you
make it feel as if you're being baptized
by Holy Water from Heaven above
let the lightning light up the dark sky
so you can see the truth
through the deceit and lies.

Uniform #11

An all-American
straight "A" student
never got in trouble
always helped others
in their time of need
was the star quarterback
for his high school football team

He tutored younger kids after school
drove his friends around town
had a job at the local super market
while leading his teams to state championships
had a loving and supporting girlfriend
a full ride scholarship to any college
that was until

One rainy Saturday night
he was on route nine
coming home from visiting his grandparents
when a truck lost control
crossed the double yellow line
and hit his car head on

Now this Friday night
at the last football game
his high school honors him
hanging his jersey in the main hallway
to a reminder to all students
life can be short.

Joe Tallarigo

Let's Pretend

They say memories last forever
pictures paint a thousand words
the good times are right around the bend
let's pretend that we're still together
and our fun times never did end

Remember our tailgating parties on Friday nights
when Julie tried out for the school plays
Jim wowed the crowds with his songs
we decorated the hall ways for homecoming
we talked about life and love in homeroom
let's pretend those days never ended

Remember the mornings at our lockers
meeting at the flagpole after school
staying out late on the weekends
talking about college and our future plans
let's pretend those days never ended

Let's pretend
we're still cheering in the stands
we're trying out for the band
dancing to our favorite songs at Prom
where did the years go
let's pretend that we're still together
and those days never ended.

Keep the Music Playing

Chapter Four

Music Revolution

Joe Tallarigo

We can't even Share a Fence

My wife invited our neighbors over
the ones I can't stand
their dogs bark all night
they host parties and never invite us
his truck is always covered in mud
his wife is always on the defense
their kids are too rambunctious
we can't even share a fence
without me getting upset

They don't sleep in on Saturday's
I've been up since dawn when he started his lawn mower
do they need to come over tonight
I guess if they leave by eight it'll be okay
I hope they like board games and Canasta
we can't even share a fence
without me getting upset

Pull out the pictures of our kids
you know they will if we don't
he and I should talk sports
but he's a fan of the rival team
you and her can talk about the latest fashions
Honey, to be perfectly honest they drive me crazy with a passion
we can't even share a fence
without me getting upset

If we continue to live next to them
can we build a ten-foot fence
so we don't have to be neighbors at all.

Family Feud

The brothers are taking over
as the sisters are being pushed aside
tradition is being thrown out the window
some are speaking out on the direction
country music is heading
but it seems to be falling on deaf ears
how did we get here from there

Grandfather and mother sit all alone
the mothers are nowhere to be found
the fathers have been silenced
the kids are forgetting their roots
there's a generation gap
of those who embrace history
and those who want change

There's nothing wrong doing your own thing
but the dirt roads and trucks can't go on forever
the pendulum will one day swing back
to the traditional sound
hopefully there won't be any cracks
in the circle

Label executives pushes what's hot and sells
even if it means casting those aside
who are deep in their careers
we all need to put aside our differences
and come together
get back to the roots
of honest storytelling
and having listeners feel something deep in their soul
I just hope it's not too late
to undo what's been done
in this family feud.

Joe Tallarigo

The Show must go On

Run down, got out of town
on this cold December night
in the glow of the Nashville neon lights
we pack up our pride, our guitars
setting out coast to coast
to play our songs to rowdy crowds

We don't want the money, going to give it to charity
we'll hang out with the locals, drink beers
play pool between shows
write our songs on the road
we never want to go back home

The show must go on
things aren't what they used to be
can't get our songs on the radio
what happened to Waylon's fight
we ignore the critics
it's all about the fans

We got creative with our image and sound
jam with our friends on stage
we call on traditionalists
to form their own record labels
to fight the system

The show must go on
things aren't what they used to be
can't get our songs on the radio
what happened to Waylon's fight
we ignore the critics
it's all about the fans.

Music Revolution

Let's find a large plot of land
gather the best singers and bands
set up a large stage with bright lights
make our own four-day musical festival
only sell tickets at the gate
we'll serve food and drinks to the guests
put aside our differences and politics
make it all about the music

Let's hear some long guitar solos
the beating of the drum that drives the song
sing about love, freedom, and hope
get loud, be daring, go crazy on stage
don't let the establishment stifle creativity
we need another musical revolution
one that will inspire a new generation of artists
like they had in the 1960's

Where are the rock and rollers
the tough country outlaws
that aren't afraid to cross the line
it seems today artists are playing it safe
following the trends and fads
we need to start taking risks
to make people question
if reality is truly black and white

We're all children of the light
living mundane lives
we need a spark to start a fire
to set off a new wave of creativity
let's not get stuck in a rut
where the music won't allow us to dance
or have meaning and substance
we need a music revolution.

Joe Tallarigo

Chapter Five

Country Standard Time

Country Standard Time

We have a real saloon
bartenders who'll listen to your problems
a jukebox that plays Hank Williams
we talk about our dogs, trucks, farms,
our exes who broke our hearts
we grow cotton and corn in our fields
put our fancy toys in red barns
so if you need to unwind
from the city life
welcome to Country Standard Time

There's all night fishing, moonlight kissing
Sunday morning church services
we have white picket fences
afternoon picnics by the river
then go out in canoes
and take a trip down stream

Do you know the importance of New Year's Day 1953
or who was in the class of 1989
who was Lefty, Waymore, The Hag, The Possum
do you know who was nicknamed The Voice
I'll give you a hint
his songs will make your tears fall into your beer
who is the king and queen of country music
if you would like to know
come have a seat
and we'll tell you the history
of Country Standard Time

Country music is more than open roads and freedom
more than prison, drinking, cheating songs
even more powerful than a love song
it's about being true to who you are
no matter where you are.

Joe Tallarigo

Back to the Basics

Let's get back to the basics
with steel guitars and songs with substance
playing them on locally owned country music radio stations
where DJ's and listeners
have a say in what's being played

Let's get back to the basics
of hanging out at night
sitting around campfires
singing about cowboy's and the wild west
and telling stories of our travels

Let's get back to the basics
of going to church on Sunday's
dressing up to go out for dinner
saying yes ma'am and no sir
and allowing prayer back in schools

Let's get back to the basics
where singers dream of gracing
the stage of the Opry
we need to honor its history
and keep the traditional country music alive

Let's get back to the basics
when all women were played on the radio
and not just the popular three
I want to hear every women's stories and songs
about love and heartaches

Let's get back to the basics
with steel guitars and songs with substance
playing them on locally owned country music radio stations
where DJ's and listeners
have a say in what's being played.

Echoes of Country Music

I hear the midnight whistle
rumbling down the line
there's ole Johnny boy
hanging out in the town square
with whiskey on his breath
while the dogs are howling at the moon

The rain is pouring
down on the brokenhearted
they are drinking down their pride
Hank is signing for them tonight
helping to heal their pain and heartache

Somewhere in the honky-tonks
the outlaws are performing their songs
about cowboys and good-hearted women
in Memphis there's a rock star
making all the girls swoon

And all across this country
people are acting out cheating songs
a rhinestone cowboy walks the streets
a mom makes a coat of many colors
for her daughter
a truck driver is trying to get home
after being out on the road for a month

These are the echoes of country music's past.

Joe Tallarigo

Writers Block

I bought new pens and paper
though I have drawers full of both
I began listening to new singers and bands
hoping to trigger my imagination
having new inspiration
I'm in a race against the clock
to finish my books
but I find myself having writers block

Staring at the blue lines on the paper
reminds me of my one track mind
writing poems only about my family and friends
I need to mix it up
come up with lyrics that stir the imagination
and make the readers question
where I came up with the ideas and words
but I feel like I'm backed against a wall
being held captive by my writers block

The minutes pass by, my dog wants to go for a walk
I'm also hungry and need a snack
but there's still no words on my paper
it's getting frustrating that my imagination
has been put on hold
when there are stories that need to be told
I need to unclog my words so they flow
to end this writers block.

The Visit

I sat in his living room chair
staring at his gold and platinum albums on his walls
I was nervous to be here
but his booming and commanding voice put me at ease
made me feel like we were old friends
when he asked me what was on my mind

I said I've been putting off my dreams
because the realities in my life
I just can't up and leave my hometown in the middle of the night
and I wouldn't know where to begin in Nashville
before I could continue, he looked me straight in the eyes
said you can do anything you like, you just need faith
I didn't become the man in black just to let my life slip away
I had a message for the broken hearted and those down on their luck
now turn that frown into a smile, you're still young
stand your ground and follow the road in your heart

I sat there in awe
he didn't know my full story, but I knew his
his words touched my soul
that's all that mattered to me
I know in my heart, God sent me to him
to help my fears and insecurities

He said I have to go now
I hope you got the advice you were looking for
he then handed me a piece of paper with a phone number on it
if you ever decide to come to Nashville
he'll help you with your goals and dreams
just like he helped me
tell him Ole Johnny Cash sent you.

Joe Tallarigo

Angels and Stars

All this world has given me
is angels and stars
appearing in my life causing synchronicity
from my love of weather, attending Oak Hills,
hanging out in Bowling Green, Ohio
and listening to country music
there are no coincidences
I was meant to meet those people and be at those places
to help guide me on my journey

There's been some bumps in my road
and heartaches that left scars
life was once a merry-go-round
always ended up where I started from
I could never get ahead
but now I'm moving forward
getting closer to where I belong
thanks to the help of my angels and stars

I'm still tapping my feet
to the beat of the drums
I still want my poems
turned into songs
having people sing along
Nashville will throw a party for me
for getting a number one hit
in my speech I'd thank my angels and stars

Angels and stars
go hand in hand
because in my darkest moments
I looked towards the sky
for the answers I seek
hoping to receive a sign
and I always happened to find
angels and stars.

Songwriter's Dream

Midnight bells ring in the distance
I'm still awake wondering what words I'll chance
to make a rhyme or two
I reflect on the good and bad times
I had with my family and friends
to write these lines

I'm living a songwriter's dream
that began in 1999
on my first day of high school
I made many new friends
that opened me to a new brand world
that changed me
I'm living a songwriter's dream

I found new inspiration
when Big and Rich, Gretchen Wilson
came bursting onto the country music scene
they introduced me to Waylon and the other outlaws
of the 1970's
helping me along in my songwriter's dream

I found love at first sight in 2004
she inspired my songwriting even more
a fire of passion began to burn
the wheels began to turn
I was on my way
in my songwriter's dream

Now here I am years later
still writing songs about my life
I wouldn't change a thing about my past
I look forward to what the future will bring
in my songwriter's dream.

Joe Tallarigo

If you like Good Music (Come Along)

If you like good music come along with me
I'm hosting one big party
you're welcome to invite all your friends
it's going to last for days
I have thousands of songs to play

I'm going to start with
Hank Jr's "All my rowdy friends are coming over tonight"
followed by Gretchen Wilsons "Here for the party"
and when the drinks are being passed out
I'll play "Margaritaville"
we'll raise our glasses and toast to this good time

If you like good music come along with me
let go of your worries
listen to the rhythm of the music
sing along to your favorite songs
let the lyrics take you to your favorite place

I'll play "Sweet Home Alabama"
"Give me three-steps"
we all know where we want to be
in the Caribbean with Kenny Chesney
or with the outlaws in the honky-tonks
with Waylon, Willie, and Billy Joe Shaver

If you like good music come along with me
I'm hosting one big party
you're welcome to invite all your friends
it's going to last for days
I have thousands of songs to play.

Unsung Country Music Singer

Down past the Mason Dixon Line
there's a young man up on stage
singing songs, he wrote
then he pays tribute to those who came before him

He drinks Jim Beam, writes about love and pain
walked the same roads as his heroes
but you won't find him on tv talking about his history
or find his cd's in the malls or hear him on the radio
he won't be on the CMA's with the other big stars
since he's local and only plays at bars
but he's a fighter and carries on
he's an unsung country music singer

He dreams of being on the Opry
playing to sold out crowds
but he never left his hometown
where little old ladies know his name
and are his biggest fans
but he hears through the wind Nashville calling him

He drinks Jim Beam, writes about love and pain
walked the same roads as his heroes
but you won't find him on tv talking about his history
or find his cd's in the malls or hear him on the radio
he won't be on the CMA's with the other big stars
since he's local and only plays at bars
but he's a fighter and carries on
he's an unsung country music singer.

Chapter 6

Music of the Angels

Sunday's

My parents took us to church at nine
best suits and dresses on
shoes had to be polished and shine
there wasn't time to waste, we couldn't be late
we had to hear the choir sing, the priest's homily
then afterwards we'd spend the afternoon
at my grandparent's house

I read the bible in my room
when other kids were playing outside
I was too busy looking for salvation in this crazy world
there's only one thing I know for sure
the sun sets in the East, rises in the West
the rest is up to God

I never saw Grandpa cry
he was a strong-willed man
who fought in two wars
never relied on God
but when grandma passed away
he laid flowers on her grave
he broke down, got on his knees
asked God for mercy and grace
to get him through the rest of his days

He's now in his best suit
singing along with the choir
he even got baptized last week
now every Sunday
we go to church and pray
as a family.

Joe Tallarigo

Music of the Angels

Every morning my friends and I
would go down to the country store
to hear Charley play his banjo
when he plucked the strings
I always believed it was

The music of the angels
echoing through the valley
I imagined them joining in
picking away on their harps
then having a drink of Strawberry Wine
as they praised God for the sound
of beautiful music being played

Aunt Patty was a religious woman
who went to church everyday
always sat in the front pew
raising her hands to Heaven
as she sang along to

The music of the angels
echoing through the valley
she imagined them joining in
picking away on their harps
then having a drink of Strawberry Wine
as they praised God for the sound
of beautiful music being played

Charley and Aunt Patty
loved to tell stories of their youths
when neighbors would gather at each other's houses
they would grab guitars and empty jugs
as someone whistled a tune
they would sing and play

Keep the Music Playing

The music of the angels
echoing through the valley
she imagined them joining in
picking away on their harps
then having a drink of Strawberry Wine
as they praised God for the sound
of beautiful music being played.

Joe Tallarigo

Roses in Heaven

Good evening God, it's good to talk to you again
I'm not here to make a request
all my earthly needs are being met
but I do have a question for you
that I need to know

Are there roses in Heaven
if there's not
can you plant some in front of my mansion
so they'll be in bloom
when I enter the Pearly Gates
and come home to you

Are the streets made of gold
how old will I be in my white robe
will I be able to hang out with my childhood friends
are there winding rivers, snowcapped mountains
but most of all

Are there roses in Heaven
if there's not
can you plant some in front of my mansion
so they'll be in bloom
when I enter the Pearly Gates
and come home to you

God, before I go
if there are roses already in Heaven
can you give one each to my family and friends
who are with you this day
so they know I'm thinking of them
and tell them I'll see them again one day.

Sunday Morning Country Song

Tonight, I'm crazy for staying up late
it's Saturday night and tomorrow I need my saving grace
sweet mama would slap me silly
for not putting my ten percent in the collection plate
but there's an urgent request
from the traditional country music fans
they don't understand why there's none being played

It's One A.M. and I'm going crazy
listening to the songs I cut my teeth on
trying to recapture that sound
but my neighbor keeps coming down
said son your guitar riffs are too loud
I'm not going to give you another warning
some of us have places to be in the morning
you need to give it a rest

The morning sun looked like a spirit of fire as it rose
I felt the grace of God as He told me
son take a shower, put on your suit and tie
go to church and I'll give you what you need
to my surprise the priest preached on changes in tradition
he said some of us adapt to this ever-changing world
some stay behind, and some want to control it

At 11:59 A.M. I was out the door
before the final amen could be said
I knew what I had to do
I mixed a little rock with the blues
and added a dash of steel guitar
to come up with this
Sunday morning country song.

Joe Tallarigo

Easter

Chocolate bunnies, jelly beans, marshmallow peeps
bubbles, chalk, baseball gloves and dolls
are placed in Easter baskets for boys and girls
outside colored eggs are hidden
for the big Easter egg hunt after church
the ham, green beans, potatoes are in the crock pot
being slow cooked for the afternoon meal
with the family

Halleluiah! Jesus has risen
shedding his blood for our sins
He's the reason for the season
let's give him all our glory and praise
on this holy day

Spring brings in renewal and birth
with flowers blooming in the gardens
warmer weather is moving in
kids are riding their new bikes in the streets
lovers are holding hands in the parks
and baseball fans are gathering in the stadiums
rooting on their favorite teams

Halleluiah! Jesus has risen
shedding his blood for our sins
He's the reason for the season
let's give him all our glory and praise
on this holy day.

Me and my brother on Easter

Joe Tallarigo

Pray Anyway

I'm going to get on my knees
close my eyes, fold my hands
and talk to God
though He already sees and knows everything
I'm going to make the case for miracles for those who need it the most
because I've seen people and their situations change
in ways I can't explain
you may not believe, that's okay
I'm going to pray anyway

I believe there are angels walking the streets
waiting for their divine appointments
to lift up people's lives more than they could ever imagine
if only more people opened their hearts and eyes
they could see there's more than bone and flesh
there's a whole spiritual realm around us
moving in ways no one can explain
they rearrange things so we can achieve our dreams

Don't ask me why bad things happen to good people
though I have my own beliefs
but I believe it's up to each individual to figure it out
prayers go up and swirl around the throne of Heaven
sometimes God says no and makes us wait
so we can appreciate what we have
and He won't give us everything what we want
but I'm going to pray anyway.

In the Palm of His Hand

I gaze up at the sunset, that's painting me a picture
of endless hopes and dreams
a warm gentle breeze brushes my face
I can't think of any place
I'd rather be
life is meant to be lived
and not be full of regrets

I'm in the palm of His hand
He has laid out my plans
I can count on Him seeing me through
the storms of life and twists and turns
His light is always shining
through the darkness of night
I know I'm only a mortal man
But He's got me in the palm of His hand

When I'm out on the sea
I feel the motion of the waves
I feel alone and scared
as the dark clouds and storms surround me
but I know He's watching me from Heaven above

I'm in the palm of His hand
He has laid out my plans
I can count on Him seeing me through
the storms of life and twists and turns
His light is always shining
through the darkness of night
I know I'm only a mortal man
But He's got me in the palm of His hand

He's all around us if we just have faith
and open our eyes to the unknown
He's all around us if we just believe
and get baptized.

Joe Tallarigo

Eastern Skies

I'm looking towards Eastern skies
I see the signs the end of times is coming nigh
and what a glorious day it's going to be
when the final trumpet blows
and out of the clouds
Jesus will appear on his white horse
and welcome us with open arms
we'll fall on our knees
ready to be taken home

I've been tested and had tribulations
people ask me how I can still believe
when God has taken so much away
but without my faith I would have gone crazy
it's true I had my share of doubts and questions
but I understand God has a plan
sometimes events have to transpire
to see his works and mysteries
He's truly my rock which I stand on

I'm looking towards Eastern skies
so I won't miss the homecoming
it's going to be a glorious day
when all my family is reunited
there'll be no more pain or sadness
no more stars, sun, or moon
it'll be all day praising
feasts with the king of kings
will you look with me
towards the Eastern skies.

Chapter Seven

My Home is the Road

Joe Tallarigo

My Home is the Road

My home has four-wheel drive
which takes me across the country
through the cities, down the back roads
I'm always on the go
until I find myself a Ma and Pa diner
then it's time for roast beef and gravy
with a slice of apple pie

I was never one to stand still
been on the move since I was nine months old
I love traveling coast to coast
seeing all the unique buildings
and the tourist traps

I make small talk at rest stops
asking travelers where they're headed
I advise them to take it slow
because it's the journey that counts
the story you'll tell for years
it's always funny when you drive
a hundred miles past your destination
and have to turn around

I was never one to stand still
been on the move since I was nine months old
I love traveling coast to coast
seeing all the unique buildings
and the tourist traps

My home has always been the road
I'm always on the go
from San Francisco to Chicago
I can say each city has its own unique flair
but I could never live there
the white lines and speed limit signs would miss me.

Pedal to the Metal

Vroom-Vroom
he puts the pedal to the metal
down the street he goes
his mother a few steps behind
yelling go-slow
only three years old, he's already on the run
he's her only son
and one day he'll be gone

With the pedal to the metal
he'll be chasing his dreams
down the highways in his truck
he'll burn up the road
with his smile and big heart
he'll make his mother proud
putting the pedal to the metal

The green flag is always waving
he loves to run around and play
as he smiles back at his mom
knowing there'll come a day
he's going to stir up the dust
with his truck
and hit the open road

With the pedal to the metal
he'll be chasing his dreams
down the highways in his truck
he'll burn up the road
with his smile and big heart
he'll make his mother proud
putting the pedal to the metal

When he gets older he'll come back and visit
give his mother a kiss on the cheek
and give up the keys to his truck
and take care of her
until then

He will put the pedal to the metal
chasing his dreams
down the highways in his truck
he'll burn up the road
with his smile and big heart
he'll make his mother proud
putting the pedal to the metal.

Midnight Stroll

I took a midnight stroll to clear my head
crickets were making sweet music like a symphony
the stars, planets, and moon were making bets
that I'd actually find peace and tranquility
on this lonesome dirt road

I took a midnight stroll
for love and heartache took their toll on me
I wore a hole in the ground
hoping you'd call me on the phone
or show back up at my front door

This road isn't so bad during the day
but when it gets dark
I don't know what's coming around the bend
especially those drivers driving back from town
they drive recklessly
after spending all night drinking to old memories

Mr. Moon can you spare me a little more light
to guide me through this heartache
so that I can find peace and tranquility
and finally get some sleep

I took a midnight stroll to clear my head
crickets were making sweet music like a symphony
the stars, planets, and moon were making bets
that I'd actually find peace and tranquility
on this lonesome dirt road.

Joe Tallarigo

Cracker Barrel

Wooden rocking chairs on the porch face the highway
a large knitted checkerboard with large checkers
is set up ready to be played
country songs from the 1950's and 1960's
are being played on the stereo
I'd like to check out the country store first
but I may run out of money buying gifts before I get to eat

Waitress, I don't need a menu I'm ready to order
I'll have the grilled chicken, green beans, macaroni and cheese
while I wait for my food to be made and brought out
I play the wooden cribbage board games with the colored pegs
like I did as a kid

I love the down-home atmosphere
couples are having conversations
the food tastes like mama used to make
you'll be filled up until you order dessert
better save some room for the pies

Now is the time to go shopping
Cd's, teddy bears, statues, chocolate candies,
DVD's, birthday cards, t-shirts
they have toys for the kids
it's hard to choose what to buy

I finally settle on the chocolate buckeye's, a classic country cd
to listen to on the way home
and next time I'll buy
a wooden rocking chair for my front porch
it gives me an excuse to visit
my local Cracker Barrel again.

Party in New Orleans

Let's party and get rowdy
you know the fun never dies down
on this side of town
someone new always comes in
bringing in a second wind
we treat them like long lost kin
show them around the French Quarter
and all that New Orleans has to offer

The string lights on the street
will never be shut off
as long as the jazz bands and steel drums
keep the musical beat going
feel the rhythm of the Caribbean and Cajun music
pulsating through your veins
you'll never want to go back home
once you visit New Orleans

The Bourbon and Tequila is always flowing
the jukebox is fired up
come dance or sing along
or sit outside with your friends on the deck
order a few rounds of crawfish and jambalaya
wear your most colorful suit and tie
catch the eyes of the dancing queens
and have yourself a night in New Orleans.

Joe Tallarigo

Carolina Gypsy Rose

Carolina Gypsy Rose you have my heart and soul
have me twisted around your little finger
but there's something you ought to know
I can't always be around
there are thousands of fans
who want me to visit their towns
and play my songs for them
it's the career I chose
but life is good Carolina Gypsy Rose

When I get back from the road
you'll get my full attention
we'll eat some ice cream
have tea parties with your friends
watch movies all day long
but when Summer comes back around
I'll be back on the road
but I'll call you everyday
my Carolina Gypsy Rose

Carolina Gypsy Rose you have my heart and soul
have me twisted around your little finger
but there's something you ought to know
I can't always be around
there are thousands of fans
who want me to visit their towns
and play my songs for them
it's the career I chose
but life is good Carolina Gypsy Rose

Carolina Gypsy Rose, I want you to know
before you came along
all I had was my songs
but I wanted a daughter more
Carolina Gypsy Rose
you have my heart and soul
and I'm your biggest fan in the world.

Chattanooga Calling

I thought I'd give you a call
I won't be home tonight after all
I left Gainesville at five
hoping to be home by midnight
but the traffic and rain slowed me down
I stopped in Atlanta at the Holiday Inn
I'll see you and the kids in the morning

I hope I can get some sleep tonight
it's hard to do
when I hear Chattanooga calling me
where you make our house a home
our girls play soccer in the yard
and our boy works with me on our cars
can't wait to hold you in my arms
going to set my alarm for Five A.M.
to get to Chattanooga by eight

I lay my head on my pillow
turn on the TV to watch the Blue-Collar Comedy Tour
I find them all pretty funny
but my wife also has a good sense of humor
and my kids like to play pranks on me
I wish I was there with them
and not stuck in this hotel

I hope I can get some sleep tonight
it's hard to do
when I hear Chattanooga calling me
where you make our house a home
our girls play soccer in the yard
and our boy works with me on our cars
can't wait to hold you in my arms
going to set my alarm for Five A.M.
to get to Chattanooga by eight.

Joe Tallarigo

Happy Birthday (I wish I was There)

It's your birthday today
wish I was there to help you celebrate
but I'm sending you a dozen roses
and a kiss from the road
tell everyone I say hello

I'm sure all our friends and family are there
with lots of presents and food
singing Happy Birthday to you
as you blow out your candles
make a wish that will come true

Being away on business is hard
I'd rather be home
and help you celebrate
please have a slice of cake for me
with a scoop of ice cream

I'll be home later this month
I'll take you to your favorite restaurant
and spend the whole day with you
one day I won't be traveling anymore
and I'll home all the time

Happy Birthday darling
I wish I was there
to help you celebrate your special day.

Starlight, Starbright, Take me home Tonight

Starlight, starbright, take me home tonight
an Amarillo girl got me to drop to my knee
it was love at first sight
I placed a diamond ring on her finger
but our love didn't last long
and she ran off with someone new

I'm stuck here heartbroken in Amarillo
with no way to get back home
to my bed in Oklahoma
tonight, I'm making wishes
on those shining diamonds
that hang high in the Texas sky

Starlight, starbright, take me home tonight
an Amarillo girl got me to drop to my knee
it was love at first sight
I placed a diamond ring on her finger
but our love didn't last long
and she ran off with someone new

A blue moon rose over the trees
the night she told me goodbye
I went straight to the bars
to drown my sorrows
hoping that one of my tomorrow's
I'll make my way back to Tulsa

Starlight, starbright, take me home tonight
an Amarillo girl got me to drop to my knee
it was love at first sight
I placed a diamond ring on her finger
but our love didn't last long
and she ran off with someone new.

Joe Tallarigo

Keychains, Postcards, and Shot Glasses

Every road trip requires a stop at a gas station
when I cross a state line
to stock up on snacks and pop
for the long drive to the hotel
I buy some scratch offs for good luck
and to browse the shelves for
keychains, postcards, and shot glasses

I like the colorful art on the
keychains, postcards, and shot glasses
I'll even buy an occasional magnet or snow-globe
with a city design in the background
when I'm in a new town
I'll be purchasing
keychains, postcards, and shot glasses

They're reminders of the trips I've been on
keychains I hang on my walls
postcards I put in albums or frames
shot glasses I put in the curio cabinet

We all have our hobbies and collections
mine just happens to be plastic and glass mementos
that won't break the bank
and I'd like to thank the artists and companies
who make the
keychains, postcards, and shot glasses.

Goodnight Vegas

Goodnight Vegas, I had a marvelous time
rolling the dice, playing the slots, drinking red wine
I lived it up the past week
trying to hit the big one

Thanks for inviting me to the party
I made some new friends
and bluffed my way through the games
I had a ball
trying to win it all

Goodnight Vegas, it's time I move on
Sinatra sang his last song
I came here in a Cadillac
now I'm leaving on a greyhound bus
but I'm not raising a fuss

The bright lights will shine on
there'll always be winners and losers
it's all for fun anyway
relying on luck and superstition
trying to hit the big one

Goodnight Vegas, thanks for the memories
I'll be back again with my foolish pride
playing the devil's games in the neon lights
I'll end up spending my last dollar
playing "Fly me to the Moon"
it'll be the last thing I do
goodnight Vegas, it sure was fun.

Joe Tallarigo

Chapter 8

Keep the Music Playing/ Celebrate Life

Keep the Music Playing

It's hard to keep the music playing
when loved ones keep passing away
we're going to miss you
walking trough these bar doors at seven
sitting on your favorite bar stool
talking to friends and strangers who came in
now we always keep two credits on standby on the jukebox
in honor of your memory
and to keep the music playing

People all the time talk about their favorite songs
and all the concerts they've been to
couples choose a love song as their first dance
as husband and wife
some listen to their favorite songs on their phones
some are still old school and listen to Cd's and the radio
music no matter how we consume it
is all around us for us to enjoy
we have to keep the music playing

Music is my lifeline
though it's getting harder for me
to write poems
when everything under the sun has been written about
but I press on
turning what I see and hear into rhymes
so people can relate to what I write
and say I've been there too
I have to keep the music playing.

Joe Tallarigo

Another Goodbye to Another Good Friend

Flowers surround the casket
pictures of their lives are on poster boards
placed on easels all across the room
tears and stories echo off the walls
can't believe we're all gathered here again
to say another goodbye to another good friend

Just last week I was hanging out
with the dearly departed
talking, shopping, and packing for our annual trip
to Myrtle Beach and Gatlinburg with our friends
but we won't postpone our trip
I know they wouldn't have wanted that
they would want us to go in their memory

It's been hell these past few years
seems like every time we catch our breath
another angel gets called home
it's been a long road
from where we started from
do the good times have to end
it seems like when we arrive at a bend
we are saying goodbye to another good friend

I walk up to the casket
bow my head, pay my respects
say I'll see you in Heaven
until then
it's another goodbye to another good friend.

Keep the Music Playing

Pepper's Song

He always woke up at Six A.M. for a bacon strip
then watched from the living room window
as my brother and I got on the school bus
he'd greet us on the porch when we got back from school
sometimes he would escape from our yard
to visit the dog across the street
at night he'd go upstairs alone
and wait for me to come to bed

He loved going for rides
he visited my aunt and uncle's farm in Kentucky
went with me to Bowling Green, Ohio for a week
and visited Maysville and Deer Creek
but his favorite road trip was to East Fork Lake
enjoying his walks in the open fields
as I took photos of deer

Through the years, he would lie on his bed
staring at me
wondering what I was doing
as I put my pencil to paper
writing my poems on my bed
I'm glad he was there to keep me company
all the nights I lived on my own

He loved getting cookies from the pet store
eating lasagna and filet minion
then one day he kept falling down
and could no longer get around
my world was torn apart
when he took his last breath
he was my pal for thirteen years.

Joe Tallarigo

Pepper

(2002-2016)

Keep the Music Playing

Joe Tallarigo

Who they Were

They were soul mates, both free spirits
you could run into them in New Orleans, Chicago
at the local and national jazz festivals
going backstage to meet the singers
they cheered for the Bengals and Saints
always wore smiles and made friends wherever they went

They collected bobbleheads, tailgated before the big games
drank at the bars during Mardi Gras
bought pins and posters as mementos
to remember the moments they shared
they sat in the best seats in the house
and were the life of the party always
having a good time

I made sure to call them every week
to talk about the Reds or upcoming concerts
didn't want to miss out on a big event
I'm a free spirit, I take after them
having good times, capturing the moments
living it up, making bets at festivals
winning and losing money all in fun

Now I have some of their mementos of the places they've been
it helps me understand, who they really were
and what meant most to them
they were soul mates, free spirits
always having a good time
and wearing smiles wherever they went.

Dave and Sue

Joe Tallarigo

New Orleans

I've yet to make it to New Orleans
guess it's not meant to be
if it's not being dealt in the tarot cards
and your friends and patrons you hung out with
might be long gone and the stories they would tell
may not be true at all
but I'm not giving up the chance or dream
to visit the Big Easy

I'll bring an 8x10 photo of you two
place it on the table
I'll order three whiskey's
toast to your memory
then throw each one back
I'll shed a tear
and play a game of darts in your honor

I haven't forgotten your gypsy souls, it still resides in me
but the wind hasn't caught my sails
so I can sail down to New Orleans
life for me is getting better, you'd be so proud
of me and our friend Joani
we're writing books left and right
touching people's lives
with the words we write

If your spirits still reside in New Orleans
wait around for me, one day I'll make it there
you can guide me around your local haunts
and I can see New Orleans through your eyes
and I can say I've been to New Orleans with you.

Joani and Robin Lacy

Robin and his wife Joani make up the Cincinnati band Robin Lacy and DeZydeco. For over thirty years they have performed all over the world and bring the Cajun music and New Orleans spirit wherever they perform.

Joe Tallarigo

Daughter of the Cajun Land

She said I have Mississippi water flowing in my veins
I've played and dug for worms in the Delta mud
been waiting for a year to turn twenty-one
to attend my first Mardi Gras
my parents think I'm still too young
to be out all night on the streets with a party crowd

My grandma was a voodoo priestess
she made dolls, performed spells,
and could predict your future
mama is a homemaker
who cooks the best spiciest gumbo and crawfish
papa plays the guitar and accordion
in a DeZydeco band
my name is Jessi
and I'm a daughter of the Cajun land

I've been to Halloween masquerade parties
dressed up as a carnival queen
you should see all the boys lined up
trying to get this southern bell's crown
using their charm and fancy words
but I only dance alone

My grandma was a voodoo priestess
she made dolls, performed spells,
and could predict your future
mama is a homemaker
who cooks the best spiciest gumbo and crawfish
papa plays the guitar and accordion
in a Dezydeco band
my name is Jessi
and I'm a daughter of the Cajun land

But you're a different kind of man
why don't you take my hand
we'll stroll down Decatur street
listen to the Dixieland bands
then visit the bayou
and watch the full moon rise
and I may even kiss you

My grandma was a voodoo priestess
she made dolls, performed spells,
and could predict your future
mama is a homemaker
who cooks the best spiciest gumbo and crawfish
papa plays the guitar and accordion
in a DeZydeco band
my name is Jessi
and I'm a daughter of the Cajun land.

Joe Tallarigo

Don't Cry for Me

I heard on the radio today
that an Opry legend passed away
his rhinestones will glitter no more
as he introduced the country singers on stage

I sat down and cried
another link to Country music past is gone
I prayed for his family and friends
that's when I heard a voice behind me say

Don't cry for me, I had a good life
let's remember the songs, the good times
they can never take that away from me
my spirit will always grace the stage
at the Opry
don't cry for me

I can only imagine the fun he had
sharing the stage with fellow legends
like Roy Acuff, Ernest Tubb, Kitty Wells
sharing in the laughs with Minnie Pearl
if only there was a Country music Heaven
where they could still share their music with us

Don't cry for me, I had a good life
let's remember the songs, the good times
they can never take that away from me
my spirit will always grace the stage
at the Opry
don't cry for me.

In Loving Memory

Mary Louise was a sweet lady
who held a weekly bible study in her house
served chips and pop to her guests
she took the time to explain a bible verse
when someone didn't understand the meaning
she had a lot of patience
and could be counted on praying for you
in your time of need
what a sad day it was
when she passed away

Now family and friends gather to pay their last respects
they all say she was the nicest lady they ever met
never said a bad thing about anyone
she was the first to do the hard work
but also knew how to have fun
she never let a dark cloud
block out the sun
today we honor her in loving memory

Henry was the local barber
enjoyed giving kids their first haircuts
always knew how to get them to sit still
when they wanted to run and hide
Bobby, Will, and James were his regulars since 1972
other people would stop in for the local news
and when he wasn't busy
he'd sit on the bench in front of his shop
and greet the people walking by
what a sad day it was
when he passed away

Now family and friends gather to pay their last respects
they all say he was the kindest man they ever met
never said a bad thing about anyone
he was the first to do the hard work
but also knew how to have fun
he never let a dark cloud
block out the sun
today we honor him in loving memory

People come and go in our lives
even if it's just for a short time
they can change the way we see the world
and we should always remember them
in loving memory.

That's Life

Circumstances may get us down
your heart may shatter
as you watch your dreams
go swirling down the drain
and you might have missed the last train out of this town
now you're stuck here for a little bit longer
but always remember

The perfect sunsets in paradise fade away
the stores we shopped at for years
suddenly announce their closing down
our favorite T.V. shows get cancelled
we're left hanging with no proper goodbye
that's life, it sucks, it stings
knowing the good times may never come back
even the brightest stars in the Milky Way burn out
never to shine again
that's life my friend

Cold tropical drinks get warm
the girl you like may get asked out
before you can turn on the charm
the strongest dams fail and burst
first place teams burn out and end up last
the best made plans can go south in a flash
God always has the last laugh

The perfect sunsets in paradise fade away
the stores we shopped at for years
suddenly announce their closing down
our favorite T.V. shows get cancelled
we're left hanging with no proper goodbye
that's life, it sucks, it stings
knowing the good times may never come back
even the brightest stars in the Milky Way burn out
never to shine again
that's life my friend.

Joe Tallarigo

Just Five Minutes

There are people I'd love to see again
even if it was just for five minutes
to say hello, how have you been
can we take another photo together
its been a short goodbye for some of my friends
and for others it seems like a lifetime ago
but at one moment in time they meant the world to me

No one ever told us that one day we would wake up
and the sun would set and the universe would shift
we would no longer be hanging out with our friends
all the fun we had together would come to an end
because they moved away or got busy with life

There are moments I wish I could relive again
to shop at Thriftway, Kay-Bee Toys, Swallens
have a grilled cheese sandwich and strawberry shake at Woolworths
all these memories are short film clips
that come and go
I wish I had five minutes to shop at these stores again

We take people and businesses for granted
we get caught up that they are on solid ground
then reality knocks them down
and they are no longer around
and were left with memories and photos

I wish I had five minutes to relive my past.

Long Live my Free Spirit

Long live my free spirit
and dreams of getting away
I hate being tied down
sometimes it's hell trying to pull my roots from the ground
I want to explore the United States
meeting new people and learning the history of different towns
I'm getting older, time is getting shorter
money means nothing to me
I'm happy being broke and free
than having a job and house that brings me misery

For the past few years I was shipwrecked
and the storms kept battering me
but now I am a phoenix rising out of the ashes
a river of words flows from my soul
through the pencil to the paper
one of these days everyone will know my name
though I don't write for fame
I just want to inspire people like my hero's

I'll always be a free spirit, I'm not going to follow the crowd
I'm going to do my own thing
eat at different restaurants, visit different state parks
chase tornado's in the heartland
I'm not meant to be tied down
or stay home, I want to be out on the road
I feel most alive traveling the highways at night
God have mercy on my future wife

Joe Tallarigo

And when my spirit finally departs from my body
I hope to play amongst the stars and planets
then dive to the deepest parts of the oceans
discovering buried treasure that was lost long ago
then I'll make my way to the pearly gates
say to Saint Peter sorry I'm so late
but I've been exploring places that I couldn't before
can you let me in now
or better yet can I roam the world as a ghost
because I believe I'll never get tired traveling the world

Long live my free spirit.

Heroes

I've been lucky enough to meet some of my childhood heroes
the ones who helped shape my life
who voiced the cartoon characters or appeared on TVs shows
and I played with their action figures
I've met the singers who sang my favorite songs
and the athletes who made me
want to get out in the fresh air
and become the best player I could be

There are some heroes I still want to meet
I hope that I'm presented with the chance
to express my gratitude and tell them what they meant to me
sharing my memories I have watching them on TV
how they expanded my imagination
and helped me make my own scenes
playing outside with my friends

Some of my heroes have passed away
it's kind of sad in a strange way
that I'll never get to meet them
but I hope those who got to meet them
told them what they meant to them
and that's good enough for me
as long as they knew they made people happy

If someone inspires you and impacted your life
or changed who you are
and they made you chase a dream
I hope you get a chance to meet that person
and tell them what they mean to you.

Joe Tallarigo

I'm Just a Dreamer

The world feels like one big playground
but I don't want to steal the show
I'm here to blend in with the crowd
and allow others to shine
I'm getting to know my fellow actors
hoping they get the part they were born to play

I'm just a dreamer
with visions of inspiration and love
while living in this world full of fire and rage
where everyone gives up on hope and faith
but on the last page of the story
there's a man with open arms
waiting to take us back home

I don't want to be in the spotlight
don't need my photo taken
that's not my style of living
I just want to hang out
with family and friends
and to continue our traditions

I'm just a dreamer
with visions of inspiration and love
while living in this world full of fire and rage
where everyone gives up on hope and faith
but on the last page of the story
there's a man with open arms
waiting to take us back home

Walking the streets of my hometown
I can't comprehend what I'm seeing
there's so much promise and progress
being held back by politicians
and I see why there's no real future
for our children.

Celebrate Life

I may shed a tear just for a moment
I'm not cold or made of stone
but I'm not going to let anyone's death bring me down
or let grief hold me prisoner as it did in the past
this time I'm going to be strong

I'm going to celebrate life
keep spreading the beauty and joy
just like you did when you met anyone
too many people are living in darkness
it's time to bring them sunshine
let them experience love
that won't ever fade away

Just because you've flown away
doesn't mean I'll quit loving you
you'll always be with me with every step I take
and if I should happen to make a mistake
I'll employ the wisdom and grace
that you instilled in me
and carry on

I'm going to celebrate life
keep spreading the beauty and joy
just like you did when you met anyone
too many people are living in darkness
it's time to bring them sunshine
let them experience love
that won't ever fade away

Time might be flying by
and we won't always have the chance
to stop and smell the roses
but I won't ever pass up a dance
or let anyone be sad or lonely

Joe Tallarigo

> I'm going to celebrate life
> keep spreading the beauty and joy
> just like you did when you met anyone
> too many people are living in darkness
> it's time to bring them sunshine
> let them experience love
> that won't ever fade away.

Finally Home

I've been through the phases of the moon
felt the emotions of the seas
went through the letters A to Z
always ended up where I began
never could cross the finish line
something always brought me back
but not this time

I broke free of my crimes
tore down my cage
I'm no longer a prisoner to guilt and shame
I feel like a kid on Christmas morning
filled with hope and joy
I walked through the doors
to a brand-new world
I'm finally home

Thought the good times were my friend
but time counted down to the bitter end
and I could no longer stand the pain and suffering
I could only put up with so much
before my spirit ran to the door
to break away

I broke free of my crimes
tore down my cage
I'm no longer a prisoner to guilt and shame
I feel like a kid on Christmas morning
filled with hope and joy
I walked through the doors
to a brand-new world
I'm finally home.

Joe Tallarigo

Hallowed Halls of Nashville

In these hallowed halls of Nashville
there are stars, guitars, plain ole country folk,
troubadours and outlaws
who shaped Country Music with songs, stories, and comedy
we can't forget their dedication and histories
one must stay quiet while standing in the round with the plaques
if you carefully listen you can hear them whisper
the circle will never be broken

In these hallowed halls of Nashville
there are nudie suits, rhinestones, cowboy hats, and boots
no life story is the same, but they all have one thing in common
they all sang their songs that touched our lives
on the Opry, Midwest Hayride, The Ozark Jubilee
you can still feel their presence
in these hallowed halls of Nashville

In these hallowed halls of Nashville
you can hear Jimmie Rogers moan the blues
you can visualize a young Kris Kristofferson and other songwriters
writing their songs in the booths at Tootsies
in these hallowed halls of Nashville
its full of people who gave their time, their lives
to share a little piece of them with us

These hallowed halls of Nashville
were built by men and women who sang a country song
without them there would be no Country Music Hall of Fame
we must remember those who passed on
some lives were cut short
but they still inspire and contributed to
these hallowed halls of Nashville.

More books from Joe Tallarigo

"Forever in my Heart~ Poems of my Youth"

"Life Goes On"

"Country Outlaws and Dark Poetry"

www.ingramcontent.com/pod-product-compliance
Lightning Source LLC
LaVergne TN
LVHW011203080426
835508LV00007B/565